WAYS TO MANAGE ANXIETY

A Reference Manual

Lorraine Watkins

Library of Congress Cataloging-in-Publication Data

ISBN: 13: 978-1983688757

Printed in the United States of America.

Dedication

I want to dedicate this therapeutic manual to those who suffer in silence with an anxiety disorder. May we as a people of the 21st century speak out loud about this mental illness as it is sweeping across our nation in mass numbers and it is no longer a taboo, but a reality that effects all of us in one way or another. We are destroyed because of the lack of knowledge and may we continue to research and find ways to manage this very difficult mental illness and not be ashamed anymore or try to sweep it under the rug no matter capacity we function in. No one is totally immune, situations change, the world around us is forever changes at rapid speed of light and with that also comes a sense of anxiety and uncertainty. It is everyone's responsibility to educate themselves about this disorder and other types of mental illness, so we can better provide healing and understanding.   I, the author wrote this book from a place of personal experience and study. I hope that it will be a beacon of light for those family members who are directly affected by the disorder. This is little manual that is used in clinics, hospitals, and colleges to enlighten us and encourage to make a difference in the word around. There is hope and ways to manage anxiety. You never have to face it alone and live in shame or embarrassment about this as we continue to find way to heal and manage it together. I hope that in better understanding these types of disorders, we can also discover ways to lower crime rates that is also sweeping the nation. My prayer is with you all and I want to in some small give hope and encouragement to my readers.

What is Anxiety?

Anxiety disorder

Anxiety disorders are a group of mental disorders characterized by significant feelings of anxiety and fear. Anxiety is a worry about future events and fear is a reaction to current events. These feelings may cause physical symptoms, such as a fast heart rate and shakiness. There are many anxiety disorders: including generalized anxiety disorder, specific phobia, social anxiety disorder, separation anxiety disorder, agoraphobia, panic disorder, and selective mutism. The disorder differs by what results in the symptoms. People often have more than one anxiety disorder.

Anxiety disorders are a group of mental disorders characterized by significant feelings of anxiety and fear. Anxiety is a worry about future events and fear is a reaction to current events. These feelings may cause physical symptoms, such as a fast heart rate and shakiness. There are a number of anxiety disorders: including generalized anxiety disorder, specific phobia, social anxiety disorder, separation anxiety disorder, agoraphobia, panic disorder, and selective mutism. The disorder differs by what results in the symptoms. People often have more than one anxiety disorder. The cause of anxiety disorders is a combination of genetic and environmental factors. Risk factors include a history of child abuse, family history of mental disorders, and poverty. Anxiety disorders often occur with other mental disorders, particularly major depressive disorder, personality disorder, and substance use disorder To be diagnosed symptoms typically need to be present for at least six months, be more than would be expected for the situation, and decrease functioning. Other problems that may result in similar symptoms including hyperthyroidism; heart disease; caffeine, alcohol, or cannabis use; and withdrawal from certain drugs, among others Without treatment, anxiety disorders tend to remain. treatment may include lifestyle changes, counselling, and medications. Counselling is typically with a type of cognitive behavioral therapy. Medications, such as antidepressants, benzodiazepines, or beta blockers, may improve symptoms.

Generalized anxiety disorder (GAD) is a common disorder, characterized by long-lasting anxiety that is not focused on any one object or situation. Those suffering from generalized anxiety disorder experience non-specific persistent fear and worry, and become overly concerned with everyday matters. Generalized anxiety disorder is "characterized by chronic excessive worry accompanied by three or more of the following symptoms: restlessness, fatigue, concentration problems, irritability, muscle tension, and sleep disturbance".

Generalized anxiety disorder is the most common anxiety disorder to affect older adults.

Panic Disorder

With panic disorder, a person has brief attacks of intense terror and apprehension, often marked by trembling, shaking, confusion, dizziness, nausea, and/or difficulty breathing. These panic attacks, defined by the APA as fear or discomfort that abruptly arises and peaks in less than ten minutes, can last for several hours. Attacks can be triggered by stress, fear, or even exercise; the specific cause is not always apparent.

In addition to recurrent unexpected panic attacks, a diagnosis of panic disorder requires that said attacks have chronic consequences: either worry over the attacks' potential implications, persistent fear of future attacks, or significant changes in behavior related to the attacks. As such, those suffering from panic disorder experience symptoms even outside specific panic episodes. Often, normal changes in heartbeat are noticed by a panic sufferer, leading them to think something is wrong with their heart or they are about to have another panic attack. In some cases, a heightened awareness (hypervigilance) of body functioning occurs during panic attacks, wherein any perceived physiological change is interpreted as a possible life-threatening illness (i.e., extreme hypochondriasis).

Agoraphobia

Agoraphobia is the specific anxiety about being in a place or situation where escape is difficult or embarrassing or where help may be unavailable. Agoraphobia is strongly linked with panic disorder and is often precipitated by the fear of having a panic attack. A common manifestation involves needing to be in constant view of a door or other escape route. In addition to the fears themselves, the term agoraphobia is often used to refer to avoidance behaviors that sufferers often develop. For example, following a panic attack while driving, someone suffering from agoraphobia may develop anxiety over driving and will therefore avoid driving. These avoidance behaviors can often have serious consequences and often reinforce the fear they are caused by.

Social anxiety disorder

Social anxiety disorder (SAD; also known as social phobia) describes an intense fear and avoidance of negative public scrutiny, public embarrassment, humiliation, or social interaction. This fear can be specific to particular social situations (such as public speaking) or, more typically, is experienced in most (or all) social interactions. Social anxiety often manifests specific physical symptoms, including blushing, sweating, and difficulty speaking. As with all phobic disorders, those suffering from social anxiety often will attempt to avoid the source of their anxiety; in the case of social anxiety this is particularly problematic, and in severe cases can lead to complete social isolation.

Social physique anxiety (SPA) is a subtype of social anxiety. It is concern over the evaluation of one's body by others. SPA is common among adolescents, especially females.

Post-traumatic stress disorder

Post-traumatic stress disorder (PTSD) is an anxiety disorder that results from a traumatic experience. Post-traumatic stress can result from an extreme situation, such as combat, natural disaster, rape, hostage situations, child abuse, bullying, or even a serious accident. It can also result from long-term (chronic) exposure to a severe stressor- for example, soldiers who endure individual battles but cannot cope with continuous combat. Common symptoms include hypervigilance, flashbacks, avoidant behaviors, anxiety, anger and depression. There are a number of treatments that form the basis of the care plan for those suffering with PTSD. Such treatments include cognitive behavioral therapy (CBT), psychotherapy and support from family and friends.

Posttraumatic stress disorder (PTSD) research began with Vietnam veterans, as well as natural and non-natural disaster victims. Studies have found the degree of exposure to a disaster has been found to be the best predictor of PTSD.

Separation anxiety disorder

Separation anxiety disorder (SepAD) is the feeling of excessive and inappropriate levels of anxiety over being separated from a person or place.

Separation anxiety is a normal part of <u>development</u> in babies or children, and it is only when this feeling is excessive or inappropriate that it can be considered a disorder. Separation anxiety disorder affects roughly 7% of adults and 4% of children, but the childhood cases tend to be more severe; in some instances, even a brief separation can produce panic. Treating a child earlier may prevent problems. This may include training the parents and family on how to deal with it. Often, the parents will reinforce the anxiety because they do not know how to properly work through it with the child. In addition to parent training and family therapy, medication, such as SSRIs, can be used to treat separation anxiety.

Situational anxiety

Situational anxiety is caused by new situations or changing events. It can also be caused by various events that make that individual uncomfortable. Its occurrence is very common. Often, an individual will experience panic attacks or extreme anxiety in specific situations. A situation that causes one individual to experience anxiety may not affect another individual at all. For example, some people become uneasy in crowds or tight spaces, so standing in a tightly packed line, say at the bank or a store register, may cause them to experience extreme anxiety, possibly a panic attack. Others, however, may experience anxiety when major changes in life occur, such as entering college, getting married, having children, etc.

Obsessive–compulsive disorder

Obsessive–compulsive disorder (OCD) is not classified as an anxiety disorder by the DSM-5 but is by the ICD-10. It was previously classified as an anxiety disorder in the DSM-IV. It is a condition where the person has obsessions (distressing, persistent, and intrusive thoughts or images) and/or compulsions (urges to repeatedly perform specific acts or rituals), that are not caused by drugs or physical order, and which cause distress or social dysfunction. The compulsive rituals are personal rules followed to relieve the anxiety. OCD affects roughly 1-2% of adults (somewhat more women than men), and under 3% of children and adolescents.

A person with OCD knows that the symptoms are unreasonable and struggles against both the thoughts and the behavior. Their symptoms could be related to external events they fear (such as their home burning down because they forget to turn off the stove) or worry that they will behave inappropriately.

It is not certain why some people have OCD, but behavioral, cognitive, genetic, and neurobiological factors may be involved. Risk factors include family history, being single (although that may result from the disorder), and higher socioeconomic class or not being in paid employment.[30] OCD is chronic; about 20% of people will overcome it, and symptoms will at least reduce over time for most people (a further 50%).

Selective mutism

Selective mutism (SM) is a disorder in which a person who is normally capable of speech does not speak in specific situations or to specific people. Selective mutism usually co-exists with shyness or social anxiety. People with selective mutism stay silent even when the consequences of their silence include shame, social ostracism or even punishment. Selective mutism affects about 0.8% of people at some point in their life.

Footnote, Diagnostic and Statistical Manual of Mental Disorders, American Psychiatry Association 5th Edition, 2013

Ways to Manage Anxiety

1. When you begin to feel anxiety coming on, you can do so deep breathing techniques from five to ten minutes. This will help to relax you and calm your nerves and integrate oxygen to your brains.

2. If you can, go take a short walk from five to twenty minutes, or change the location where you are can re-energy you physically and mentally, so you can regroup and focus on something positive.

3. Talk to someone either in person or over the phone to express how you are feeling. Sometimes feedback from a friend or trusted co-worker or neighbor can be therapeutic in alleviating anxiety and panic attacks.

4. You may think you are having a heart attack when the anxiety escalates, in some cases, you may need professional intervention such as therapist or counselor to talk to.

5. If it is an everyday occurrence, you may also need to see either a licensed psychiatrist together with a licensed psychologist to help you manage your anxiety. They have help you identify triggers and causes of your symptoms.

Remember you are not alone, there are millions of Americans who suffer with anxiety disorders caused by numerous reasons. Some are caused by traumatic experiences like sexual assault, military combat experiences, and by genetic of no-fault of your own. Take heart, there are experts available to help remedy and manage this condition. Another way to manage your anxiety is to exercise and meditate of positive experiences and feelings. This is easier said than done is some cases, but has been proven to be effective.

If your doctor determines that you need medication, take it as directed and do not stop taking them without your doctor's consent and if you experience reverse side effects, do not hesitate to call your doctor or dial 911 right away.

Group therapy is also very effective in small groups of people who also live with anxiety disorders. Knowing that you are not alone make dealing with this disorder less painful and or embarrassing. There is nothing to be embarrassed about because it continues to effect millions of people each day in America and around the world.

Some people who suffer with anxiety find it difficult to manage day to day routine daily living skills such as house cleaning and cooking. It can be so debilitating that you find yourself feeling so overwhelmed and all alone. It can be so devastating that a person cannot hold down a job or have gainful substantial employment and must seek disability benefits to take care of their financial obligations. Another simple task that you may be able to do especially if you live alone is to doodle on paper, drawing lines, circles, or writing your name or small quotes that will empower you, so you can gain your posture and self-control.

You need a positive distraction like reading a book even if you only read a few pages at a time, do a simple chore even if it's a few dishes at a time. Move at your own pace and breath or stretch your muscles for relaxation.

Eating a healthy diet is just as important as exercising; these components are important to improving your overall health.

In most cities around the country, there are social and treatment centers who have a list of community activities that you can participate in and or volunteer your time. This is very helpful in creating a stronger sense of self, elevating your self-esteem, and self-confidence.

Try not to take on too many obligations at one time and know that its okay to say no or to change your mind if you are simply not up to the task. You will not be penalized for it. Work and play at your own pace and find something that you enjoy doing that is beneficial to improving your health and your self-esteem.

They maybe times throughout your life that you may need to be hospitalized temporarily or overnight just to stabilize your condition. Do not be alarmed because sometimes it is necessary and medical qualified professionals are available to assist you to make you feel better overtime.

Some people say that the best way to overcome your fears is to face them head on; but I caution you that in some cases, it is true, but not all size is the same measure for all people. Find our what works for you and don't feel like you must prove something to someone else that you are proficient, or enough. You are enough just like God made you.

Remember that life is a challenge for all of us and alone the way of this life journey, we all have our own gifts, talents, and purpose in the earth. You were created equally and or inadvertently fearfully and wonderfully made in the image of God for a higher purpose than the average person. This is a good thing because the things we experience in our life time is not only for God's purpose, but to accomplish your purpose in the earth and to help others overcome the same obstacles. So, you are a gift to others as we all are in our own way. Count it a privilege to have a higher calling and purpose in your life that is so uniquely fashioned and knitted to your inner physical and spiritual specifications.

Physical symptoms often include excessive <u>blushing</u>, <u>excess sweating</u>, <u>trembling</u>, <u>palpitations</u>, and <u>nausea</u>. <u>Stammering</u> may be present, along with rapid speech. <u>Panic attacks</u> can also occur under intense fear and discomfort. Some sufferers may use <u>alcohol</u> or other <u>drugs</u> to reduce fears and inhibitions at social events. It is common for sufferers of social phobia to self-medicate in this fashion, especially if they are undiagnosed, untreated, or both; this can lead to alcoholism, eating disorders or other kinds of substance abuse. SAD is sometimes referred to as an *illness of lost opportunities* where "individuals make major life choices to accommodate their illness".

Anxiety is a normal reaction to stress and can be beneficial in some situations. It can alert us to dangers and help us prepare and pay attention.

Anxiety disorders differ from normal feelings of nervousness or anxiousness and involve excessive fear or anxiety. Anxiety disorders are the most common of mental disorders and affect more than 25 million Americans. But anxiety disorders are treatable, and many effective treatments are available. Treatment helps most people lead normal productive lives.

This is one of many topics that we should continue to talk about around the table at home and in our work places. Awareness is empowering.

About the Author

Lorraine Watkins is a 17th time author since 2010. She is a native of Albemarle, North Carolina and a graduate of Gardner-Webb University who majored in Human Services earing her BS degree late in life due to her own personal battle with mental illness and social anxiety. She continues to research, teach, and speak to small groups and individuals about these types of disorders and how that effect families and relationships.

She is also the author of "The Burden & Blessing of Being Black: The Journey." Currently she resided in the beautiful city of Greenville, South Carolina near the mountain of Asheville, North Carolina where she enjoys the simple things of life and writing books and or speaking to community groups about this topic and many more to empower, educate, and uplift the spirits of the people.

If you know someone who is experiencing any of the symptoms listed in this short manual, please get help for them right away.